relationship^{TM}

guys:
being best
friends

Bridget Heos

rosen publishing's
rosen
central®

New York

Published in 2013 by The Rosen Publishing Group, Inc.
29 East 21st Street, New York, NY 10010

Copyright © 2013 by The Rosen Publishing Group, Inc.

First Edition

Library of Congress Cataloging-in-Publication Data

Heos, Bridget.
Guys: being best friends/Bridget Heos.—1st ed.
    p. cm.—(Relationships 101)
Includes bibliographical references and index.
ISBN 978-1-4488-6832-2 (library binding)—
ISBN 978-1-4488-6835-3 (pbk.)—
ISBN 978-1-4488-6839-1 (6-pack)
1. Friendship. 2. Boys—Psychology. 3. Interpersonal relations. I. Title.
BF575.F66H465 2012
155.3'32925—dc23

                                                    2011043225

Manufactured in the United States of America

CPSIA Compliance Information: Batch #S12YA: For further information, contact Rosen Publishing, New York, New York, at 1-800-237-9932.

CONTENTS

introduction

Friendship is a powerful thing. It lets you know that you're not alone and allows you to see things in new ways. A friend is someone you can play with and talk to. Beyond that, a friend is there for you when you get hurt, face hardship, or lose a family member. For that reason, friendship is more about quality than quantity. It's great to have lots of friends, if that's your style, but it's also OK to have just one. Even if you do have lots of friends, it's important that you can confide in and rely on at least one of them.

You may be reading this surrounded by friends—maybe friends you've known since kindergarten. Or you may be in a new school and need to start over. Or perhaps you just don't have the good friends that you would like to have. Whatever your present situation, everybody, at some point, has to make new friends. Making friends may be second nature to you. If it's not,

don't worry. Making friends— and keeping them—are skills that can be learned.

In this book, you'll learn how to make acquaintances by striking up conversations. Next, you'll learn how to turn acquaintances into friends. If you're having trouble making friends, chapter one will also help you be the best guy you can be. You don't have to be "a cool kid" to have friends. Being a good guy will allow you to form good friendships in the long run. In chapter two, you'll learn how to nurture a friendship and be there for a friend in need. Chapter three will address problems in friendships and how to resolve them. Finally, chapter four will address a new kind of "friend," as in a social networking contact. You'll read about Internet safety and the protocol teens follow. For instance, do you wonder who you should "friend" and what you should post? In chapter four, you'll learn that and more.

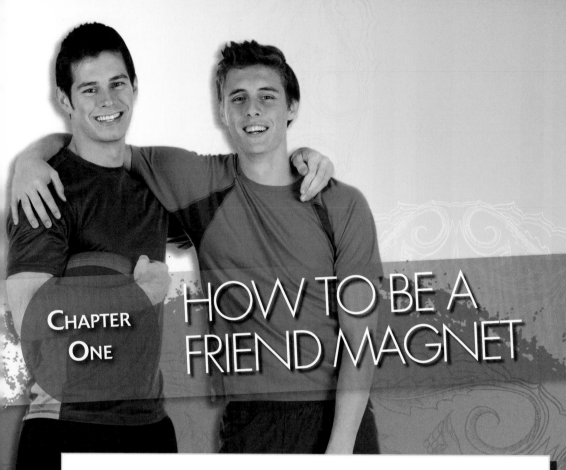

CHAPTER ONE

HOW TO BE A FRIEND MAGNET

The first step in making friends is being friendly. Say hi to people, using their names if possible. If you're shy, try this: for one week, smile when you walk down the hall or enter a room. It doesn't have to be a big, goofy smile if that's not your style. A small smile and hello to those you pass are fine.

The second step is being active. Guys often become friends because of common interests. A sport, club, or hobby is a great way to meet guys who enjoy the same things you do. If you like something that everybody else is doing, that's great. If not, decide whether you want to do something you dislike with people you know or something you like with people you don't know. If you choose the first, do your best. Be a good cheerleader for your other

Working together toward a common goal, such as winning a tournament, putting on a play, or producing a school newspaper, is a great way to develop a friendship.

teammates. If you choose the second, you'll likely meet people whom you will have more in common with. You'll have the satisfaction of working together on something you enjoy. Sometimes you don't even need to join anything. If other guys see you drawing, you might find out that they like to draw, too. Now you have something to do together. You can draw during recess or after school and share magazines that inspire you.

You can also meet friends by being involved in your community. It's fun to make friends with kids outside of school. It allows you to be yourself in a new way. Sometimes people you've known a long time think of you as the person you used to be. But you've changed in small ways through the years. When you meet someone new, he or she sees you for who you are right now.

When you first meet people, they're acquaintances. Some acquaintances never become more than that. You can still enjoy talking to them and hanging out with them. But you may feel that you don't have much in common or don't connect in terms of your personalities. You may even feel that the other person wouldn't be a good friend. Some warning signs of a potentially bad friend are:

- Dishonesty
- Risky behavior
- Talking badly about others
- Making empty promises
- Always looking for someone better to talk to
- Using people for whatever he needs without really be friends with them
- Being self-absorbed

In spite of being nice guys, some acquaintances will remain acquaintances. Others will become friends. You'll seek

Some acquaintances remain just that. Others, as you get to know each other better, become good friends. Among those friends, you'll likely have just one best friend.

each other out, rather than only hanging out when you're thrown together.

Just Acquaintances or True Friends?

When you're playing with, working with, or talking to people, you get to know them. You hear their stories, find out what they read or watch on television, discover what they think is funny, and learn what kind of teammates they are. Some of this may seem like superficial stuff, but together, it gives you a picture of who somebody is.

You start to see that you have more in common with some kids. This may be:

- Similar interests
- Similar sense of humor
- Similar values
- A shared history
- A shared situation

If you sense a connection, initiate the friendship. If you find out someone likes baseball, ask him to play a pickup game or watch a game on television. Or simply talk baseball with him. If you have a similar sense of humor, joke around with the

FIVE GO-TO CONVERSATION STARTERS

When you don't know anyone in a room, it can feel awkward. So get to know someone by striking up a conversation. If you're not sure what to say, try one of these five go-to conversation starters.

1. Compliment him and ask a question—"Congratulations on getting first in the robotics tournament. How long have you been in the robotics club?"

2. Ask his opinion—"What did you think about the Chiefs' trade?"

3. Ask him for advice—"Have you played James in chess? What opening did you use?"

4. Ask an off-the-wall question—"If you could fly or be invisible, which would you be?" "Who's a better quarterback—Eli Manning or Tom Brady?"

5. Admit a minor insecurity—If you're new at school: "Before this, I went to the same school for five years, so it's weird to look around the class and not recognize anybody. How long have you gone to school here?"

When the other guy responds, listen for things you have in common or that you could talk about later. Next time, you'll have a starting point for your conversation.

guy. If you feel you have similar values, get his take on something that happened at school. Let him know that you have a shared history, if that's the case. If you're in a shared situation, talk to him when you have the chance. If you feel like you could be friends outside of the situation, ask him over.

By now, you can probably tell if you hit it off. If you do, invite your friend to come over, go someplace with your family, or play a game as a group. This will help you get to know each other better. If you don't hit it off, the best scenario is for both of you to realize it. If he wants to be better friends than you do, be nice but limit the number of times you say yes to getting together. Gradually, he'll see that you didn't hit it off as well as he thought. Watch for these cues yourself, too. Never pursue a friendship with someone who doesn't want to be friends. You'll look desperate, and you're better than that.

You'll also waste time that could be spent finding a real friend.

On the other hand, sometimes a person needs a friend. He may not be your ideal friend. But he has no other friends. You may decide to be a friend to him. You don't have to spend every minute together. But make a point to ask how he's doing every day. Include him when he's by himself.

You may be thinking, "It all sounds so easy. Why am I having a hard time making friends?" If that's the case, first, don't take it too hard. It may be your unique situation. Are you at a new school? Do the kids you're around seem open to making new friends? It may be that they're the ones who have trouble making friends. Find people who will meet you halfway. On the other hand, is it possible that you don't want to be friends with the people you're around? Maybe you have nothing in common. Maybe you don't like how they act. If this is true, move on to a new group. Join activities and be friendly. Sometimes it takes a while to find a good friend, especially if you haven't had to make one since kindergarten. But it will happen in time.

Second, it's harder for some people to make friends than others. You may be shy. You may feel nervous around other people. You may be a little unconventional and not fit in everywhere. You may be picky about whom you want to befriend. These situations require patience. You will find a friend. And that friend will be just as valuable as the friends others made easily—maybe more so.

A third explanation is that you may need to work on yourself. This doesn't mean changing who you are. You may be tempted to act like the popular kids in the class. That strategy won't work in the long run. People can tell when you're trying too hard to fit in.

Also, being someone else is unnecessary. To have friends, you only need to be a good guy. To find out if you're being the best "good guy" you can be, answer these questions honestly:

Are You Approachable?

When you appear to be confident, you're approachable. Do you smile and say hi to people? Do you present yourself as being confident (even if you don't really feel that way)? You can look confident by looking your best, standing tall, smiling, and making eye contact. Being friendly also makes you approachable. Do you try to get to know people? The best conversationalists are good listeners. They ask questions and share thoughts. Finally, friendly people grab doors for others. Even if you're shy, lending a helping hand is a good way to be friendly.

To make friends, you need to be a good guy. Bullying is not only wrong but also makes it impossible to develop any real friendships.

Are You a Nice Guy to Be Around?

At the very least, you should never bully or exclude others. This is not only hurtful but will also make it difficult to make friends. But being nice isn't merely the opposite of being mean. Rather, nice people go out of their way to be kind. They have good manners, play fair, and keep their tempers in check. They make good choices and act responsibly. They make an effort to get along with people. Obviously there are things you could never agree with. But if you argue with everything people say, it makes you hard to talk to. The same goes for bragging, exaggerating, and acting like a know-it-all.

Are You True to Yourself?

Being nice doesn't mean being a pushover or following the crowd. Instead, you should stand up for yourself and be true to your values. While it's best to talk to people about their interests (remember the best conversationalists are the best listeners), it's important to have your own interests. Don't hide them, even if they are different from everybody else's. The point is that you're interested in something, and interested people are interesting.

Being approachable, kind, and true are three qualities that draw good friends to you over time.

CHAPTER TWO

HAVE A FRIEND; BE A FRIEND

In time, you and your friend, or perhaps a small group of friends, may become best friends. You might wonder how you can tell when somebody is your best friend. A best friend:

- Supports you in your endeavors
- Challenges you to be your best
- Listens and helps when something goes wrong
- Lets you be yourself

- Has your back
- Is somebody with whom you have fun
- Is whom you'd choose to hang out with more than anybody, except perhaps your family

Not all of your friends will be your best friends. But they can still be good friends.

When you first become friends, everything may seem perfect. You have somebody to play with and talk to. You "get" each other. At this point, the friendship may require little effort. But as time passes, you have to work on the friendship. Make time for your friend by asking him to get together or stopping to say hi at school. Ask him about things that are going on in his life. For instance, if he tried out for band, ask if he's heard anything yet. If he makes the cut, celebrate with him. If he doesn't, let him know that you're sorry. Also, always remember his birthday and holidays, and keep up-to-date on what's going on in his family.

You should also share thoughts with each other. Friends can validate your observations and beliefs. They let you know that you're not crazy; other people think that way, too. At the same time, friends can help you see things differently. When your friend is honest with you, he won't always give you the answer you're seeking. For instance, if you're mad at someone, he might say you're overreacting.

Friends care about what's going on in each other's lives. They remember birthdays and holidays and ask questions about each other's interests and goals.

Or he might suggest that if you'd studied, you wouldn't have failed the test. These things are hard to hear. But sometimes, they're just the honesty you need.

Other times, support is what's needed. If your friend is having trouble with a subject, offer to help him study. If he stays home sick, call to see how he's doing. If someone's giving him a hard time, stand up for him. If there's trouble at home, listen to him. If there's a death in his family, go to the wake and ask your parents to help you prepare a meal for

WAYS TO HELP A FRIEND IN NEED

- *Bring him his homework.*
- *Call to see if he's OK.*
- *Go over to his house and watch television with him.*
- *Ask him if he wants to throw the ball around. This will give him a chance to talk if he wants to.*
- *If he really wants to be left alone, let him, but check in within a couple of days.*
- *If you're worried about his well-being, share your concerns with his parents.*
- *If someone is sick in his family, tell your mom or dad. They can help you help his family.*
- *If he's injured or in the hospital, let classmates know, with his permission, how he's doing and how they can reach out to him.*
- *If he likes company, have classmates sign up to visit on certain days.*

the family. Being honest, being supportive, and being there when he needs you is what separates a best friend from a friend.

Not a Girlfriend, but a Friend Who Is a Girl

A girlfriend and a friend who is a girl are totally different things. A friendship with a girl will likely start in the same manner as a friendship with a guy. You'll see that you have something in common, you'll spend more time together, and you'll get to know each other better. Before you know it, you're best friends.

It's possible that you won't be in the same group of friends because she might have a group of girlfriends, and you, a group of guy friends. But you might be in a mixed group of boys and girls. Or you might be part of her group of girls, or she a part of your group of

guys. If you do have separate groups of friends, you'll have to make an effort to spend time together. However, you'll both be able to talk about problems within your group of friends, as long as you are both discreet.

You may talk about different things with your girl friend than you do with your guy friends. Boys tend to talk about things they read, see, and hear. They may talk sports, superheroes, or cars, for instance. Girls tend to talk about relationships and people. They might want to talk about kids at school or their families. Together, the two of you may talk about both. You may also talk about girls you like, and she may talk about boys she likes. Each of you can offer the perspective of the opposite sex.

You'll likely notice that your girl friend is different from you. Though every girl and every boy is an individual, most people believe that boys and girls, as a rule, differ in some

Some of the best friendships are between a girl and guy. If you have a group of guy friends, and she has a group of girl friends, you'll need to make time for each other, too.

ways. Good girl and guy friends accept those differences. Likewise, your friendship with a girl may differ from your friendship with other guys. In their friendships with each other, girls tend to be more affectionate, confiding, and nurturing, whereas boys focus on similar interests, competition, and having fun. Your friendship with a girl could skew in either direction. You may find a girl to be more

receptive to sharing feelings, or she may want a more lighthearted friendship based on playing and having fun. Or it may be a friendship completely unique to the two of you.

People may ask if you're boyfriend and girlfriend. This might be annoying, but just say, "No, we're friends." A friendship between a boy and a girl doesn't have to end romantically, no matter what you've seen on television and in movies.

CHAPTER THREE

NOBODY—AND NO FRIENDSHIP—IS PERFECT

Eventually, you'll notice that your friend isn't perfect. He'll notice the same thing about you. So how do you find common ground? Here are some common friendship problems and possible solutions.

You Realize You Have Different Interests

You may sort of like video games, so you happily played them with your friend for a while. But you'd rather play football or baseball outside. And your friend isn't really an outdoors person. In this case, see if you can you take turns. If you like being around each other, it's a good idea to compromise. At the same time, boys tend to make friends with boys who share their interests. You both may eventually gravitate toward other friends.

Many guy friendships are based on common interests. If you like to do different things and still want to be friends, you'll need to reach a compromise.

You're Annoyed by Him

If your friend is doing something that's bothering you, like bugging you about a girl or bragging about something he has that you don't, ask him to stop. If he doesn't, you may decide to take a break for a while. If little things he does bug you, you're probably spending too much time together. Take a short break.

Keep in mind that people are entitled to their quirks, even if they're slightly annoying. If there's something you really think your friend should change—because it's making him look bad or bothering others, you can bring it up, but tread lightly. At the very least, talk to him about it privately, not in a group. (Don't stage a "You need to use deodorant" intervention, for instance. Just tell him on your own.)

Your Friend Does Something Really Bad

If your friend does something rude, mean, or unethical, and you feel like it's out of character, talk to your friend. People make mistakes, and friends can call each other out when they do. If things don't change, you'll have a tough choice. Can you still be friends with this person when he acts this way? Will it affect how you act? You may need to part ways until your friend comes around.

You Have Different Ideas of What It Means to Be a Friend

You both bring unique personalities to the friendship. One of you may be an introvert (a person who derives energy from being alone) and the other an extrovert (a person who derives energy from being

Fighting with a friend can create a feeling of loneliness. But it may result in a better understanding of each other and a stronger friendship.

23

around people). Whereas the extroverted friend may want to hang out all the time, the introvert may need more time to himself. Likewise, some people are more comfortable sharing thoughts than others. This may affect what you tell each other. Finally, values can vary. For instance, some guys would defend a friend even if he was wrong. Others would tell the friend to own up to being wrong. Some guys would compete vigorously against their best friend. Others would try to work together. Some people think arguing is part of relationships. For others, too much conflict signals the end of a friendship. Think about your values and observe your friend's values. Notice that both sets of values have strengths and weaknesses. Both should be respected. Sometimes a value difference can end a friendship. Other times, the friendship is worth saving, and you must find common ground.

You Get In an Argument

No friendship is perfect. Sometimes you'll argue. You might argue about the outcome of a game, something he said, or the way you acted in a group. When you argue, it's best to find a resolution. You can let things cool down a little. But if you let the argument simmer and then forget about it, it will only bubble up again later. If you did something wrong, say you're sorry. If you think your friend did something wrong, tell him what you're mad about. Together, you may decide to do things differently next time. For instance, you may want to establish "house rules" before playing a game. The important thing is not to let negativity be the norm.

Sometimes there are issues that seem harder to work through. At this point, ask yourself if the problem can be solved. This requires honesty.

What will you need to do to solve it? What will your friend need to do, and is he willing or able to do that? Finally, if the problem isn't solved, can you live with the friendship the way it is? If not, you may decide to end the friendship or let it fade.

If you want the friendship to end but your friend doesn't, you can gradually end it by doing less together. This is less of a blow than "breaking up" with a friend. If you do tell your friend the friendship needs to end, let him know that it's not about him being a bad guy but about the friendship itself being the problem. You might say, "As friends, I think we get in trouble. I think we'd both get in less trouble if we spent less time together." When a friendship ends, take the high road. Continue to be friendly and respectful to the friend. If people ask what happened, you can tell the truth. But be as compassionate to your friend as possible.

Losing a friend can feel lonely, especially if it's your best friend. Keep in mind that you'll find another friend, and so will your old friend. Don't dwell on what went wrong. Do think about how you'd like your next friendship to be different.

Groups, Cliques, and Circumstances Beyond Your Control

Being in a group of friends can be fun. You have enough guys to play Wiffle ball. You have lots to talk about. And as each of you meets new people, you'll widen your circle of friends. But within the group, conflicts may arise. For instance, some members may be closer than others. Say you and three other guys are best friends. One summer, three of you play baseball and the other doesn't. The fourth friend feels left out. In that case, try to include your friend whenever

Being in a group of friends can be fun. You have enough guys to play basketball or football, and you always have somebody to hang out with. It can also present challenges though.

possible. If the three of you are going for ice cream after baseball, ask him to meet you there. If he's participating in something other than baseball, arrange for the three of you to attend one of his events.

When two friends in the group aren't getting along, that can cause problems, too. It may be tempting to take sides. But that only makes the problem grow. It's better to recognize the problem as just between the two friends. You can ask them to make up. But it's up to them to decide when and how to do that.

Another problem in a group is that it's hard to reach a consensus. When deciding, for instance, what to do on Saturday night, it's important to hear everybody's opinion. If you're open to all ideas, you may see that one idea is the best. If you still can't decide, you may want to take a vote, or agree to each do your own thing.

Finally, your group might exclude others. While boys tend to accept new friends, groups sometimes operate like an exclusive club. In this case, the group is a clique. You may choose to be friends with kids outside of the clique. Let the group know that you'd like them to be open-minded to new friends. Tell them why you like these people and why you'd like to see the group be more welcoming. Regardless of their decision, continue to spend time with non-clique friends.

Sometimes friendship problems arise because of circumstances out of your control. If a friend moves or changes schools, you'll naturally see less of each other. Luckily, there are lots of ways to stay in touch: e-mail, texting, social networking, or an old-fashioned letter. You can also make plans to visit him in his new city or for him to visit and stay with you. With some friends, you'll find that no matter how much time passes, you'll pick right back up where you started. Other friends tend to drift apart. In that case, rest assured that both of you will make new friends.

There are also challenges when both of you move to a new school. In middle school, you find yourself among new faces. You may seek out different activities and friend-ships. If you're both open to change, your friendship can endure the middle school turmoil. It's a good idea to have a common meeting ground so that you don't lose touch. For instance, you might eat lunch or walk home together. However, if one or the both of you feel like you don't have much in common anymore, you may drift apart. This is a tough situation. Be open to new friendships but keep in touch with your old friend. As time passes, you may find that things haven't changed so much after all.

CHAPTER FOUR

FRIENDING FRIENDS

Today, "friend" has a second meaning: someone you connect with on Facebook. Facebook is just one of many social networking sites, but it's currently the most popular. The minimum age to join sites like Facebook, Twitter, and Myspace is thirteen. Some kids lie about their age to join the sites. If you do this, your parents will likely find out from family members who are also members. Also, you won't likely have many friends on Facebook until you're thirteen. Instead, you'll wind up being friends with your friends' parents, which your friends may find awkward. That being said, thirteen isn't a magical age when you're suddenly ready for social networking. You'll want to weigh the plusses and minuses first.

On the positive side, it's a good way to stay in touch and get to know new people. If

The minimum age for many social networking sites is thirteen. You may want to look at a parent's or friend's newsfeed (with their permission) first to see what it's all about.

you're in a class with a new girl, you can send her a friend request. Based on her pictures and status updates, you'll have things to talk about. Social networking also allows you to share information.

On the other hand, social networking can be time-consuming, awkward, stressful, and troublesome. The most time-consuming part of social networking is getting started. You must decide what information to share about yourself, and send and respond to several friend requests. Later, you may find yourself checking social media sites several times a day, when you'd rather—or should—be doing something else.

The awkward part of social media is deciding what to share and dealing with others who overshare. First, you should assume that everybody you know will see your posts. Half of American adults now use social networking sites like Facebook, Myspace, and

Social networking can help you connect to others but can also cause stress if you feel you are being bullied by acquaintances online. Talk to a trusted adult, like a guidance counselor, if you need help.

LinkedIn, according to an August 26, 2011, report by the Pew Research Center. If you join Facebook, some of your first friend requests will likely come from older relatives. If you post, "Who wants to play kickball?" your grandmother might jokingly comment, "I do!" If you post, "Seventh grade mixer this Saturday," your aunt might respond, "Hope you're taking that cute girl from your football game." So be ready for that.

By now it probably goes without saying that you shouldn't post anything that would embarrass you or get you in trouble. But you can't control what other people post. If someone overshares on your wall, you can delete their comment, but others may see it first. Likewise, someone might "tag" you in a less-than-flattering photo. This allows your Facebook friends to see the photo. You can set your privacy settings to require photos to be

approved by you before they appear on your page. However, the photo, with your name, may still appear elsewhere.

Aside from awkwardness, Facebook can lead to real trouble. Kids have been bullied on Facebook and accused of bullying by their schools based on Facebook posts. If you are worried about things being posted online, let your parents know. Cyberbullying is the act of one teen or child harassing, threatening, or embarrassing another online. If you are being bullied by someone at your school, tell your school principal or guidance counselor. Even if the bullying happens outside of school, it can affect your well-being at school. For this reason, your school likely has an online bullying policy. Be careful about what you post, too. Even jokes can be interpreted as bullying if several people comment and the other

FICTION'S BEST BEST FRIENDS

What do you think of the following friends in books, in movies, and on television? Are they good friends? What do they do to show (or not show) their friendship? And are Tom and Jerry friends or enemies? Choose your favorite friends in each bracket. Continue this until you have a best friend champion.

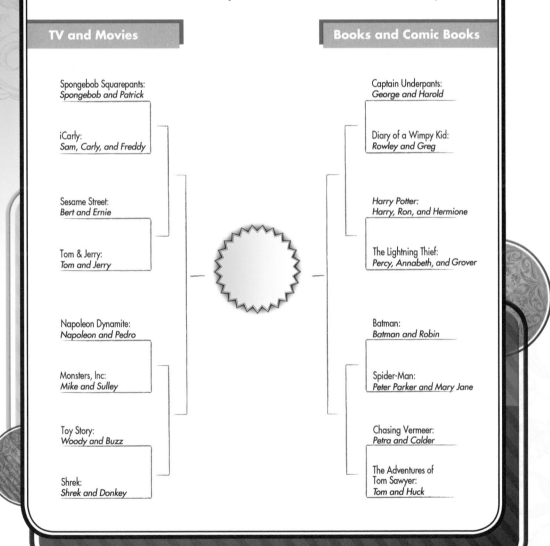

TV and Movies

Spongebob Squarepants:
Spongebob and Patrick

iCarly:
Sam, Carly, and Freddy

Sesame Street:
Bert and Ernie

Tom & Jerry:
Tom and Jerry

Napoleon Dynamite:
Napoleon and Pedro

Monsters, Inc:
Mike and Sulley

Toy Story:
Woody and Buzz

Shrek:
Shrek and Donkey

Books and Comic Books

Captain Underpants:
George and Harold

Diary of a Wimpy Kid:
Rowley and Greg

Harry Potter:
Harry, Ron, and Hermione

The Lightning Thief:
Percy, Annabeth, and Grover

Batman:
Batman and Robin

Spider-Man:
Peter Parker and Mary Jane

Chasing Vermeer:
Petra and Calder

The Adventures of
Tom Sawyer:
Tom and Huck

person feels like a target. Err on the side of caution.

A second serious concern is privacy. As a minor, you need to protect your privacy even more so than adults on Facebook. Never give out your home address. Never agree to meet someone you've met online. Don't post inappropriate pictures of yourself or others. It's rare, but some grownups do use social networking to prey on minors. Finally, be aware of your family's privacy, too. You may want to tell people about your upcoming trip to the beach, but your parents won't want everybody knowing that your house is empty.

The Social Network

If you decide to join a social networking site, you'll be asked to share information about yourself. You don't have to fill out the entire questionnaire. Share only what you and your parents think is appropriate. Next, you'll connect with people.

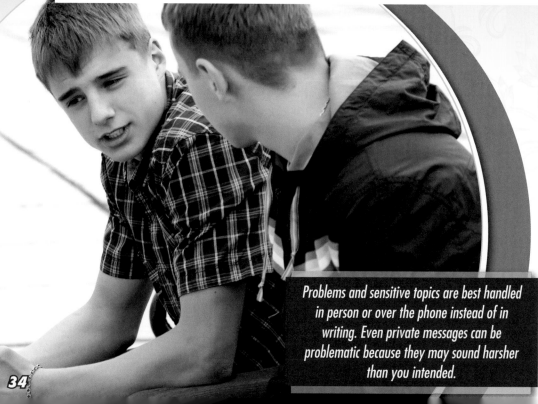

Problems and sensitive topics are best handled in person or over the phone instead of in writing. Even private messages can be problematic because they may sound harsher than you intended.

On Twitter, you do this by following people. Twitter posts are public. Anyone can look up your name and read your posts. You are allowed to join under a pseudonym, however. People use Twitter to follow celebrities, gather news, and share thoughts with friends. Among teens, Twitter is considered a more appropriate place to share random thoughts than Facebook. Posts on Twitter are fleeting, so people miss most random thoughts. On Facebook, posts linger and people get tired of reading the same random thought in their newsfeed.

Facebook requires you to use your real name. You ask people to be your "friend" and if they say yes, you can read each other's posts in your newsfeeds. You can set your privacy settings to allow only friends to see your wall and your information. Myspace is similar to Facebook. However, since Facebook is currently more popular, it will be used to describe this type of social network.

Teens generally send and accept friend requests to people they know or know of. For instance, you may get a friend request from an eighth grader at a neighboring school. You've never talked to him, but you know he plays soccer. It's up to you whether to accept these kinds of requests. If you ignore the request, the person likely won't notice. People who send requests to people they barely know tend to send a lot of requests. If eight out of ten people confirm the friendship, they'll likely forget about the other two. By the same token, if you know who the person is and he's your age, it's probably harmless to accept the friend request.

You'll likely connect with cousins, aunts, uncles, and grandparents, and Facebook is a good way to share photos and news with out-of-town relatives. You may also become friends with friends' parents or teachers (though some schools and states have policies against this). No matter how selective you are with your friends, you should consider anything you post to be public. Even if inaccessible online, it can easily be printed and shared. By the time you apply for a college scholarship or job, you'll likely have an online trail. Make sure it's a positive one. Afford your friends the same consideration. If your friend is making an obscene gesture, don't post that photo. Likewise, never post embarrassing videos or private information about people.

On Facebook, things to post include photos of you and your friends or family, fun things you're doing (headed to a game), opinions (what you thought of the game), questions (anybody know where I can get my laptop fixed?), and funny or interesting things

that happen to you. If you babysit or mow lawns, Facebook is also a great place to share information about your business. It's normal to post a couple of times a day, but you don't have to post that often, or at all. Whereas you may have hundreds of friends, teens typically only comment on or like their good friends' day-to-day posts. However, even distant friends appreciate a happy birthday message or congrats on big news they share.

The key to Facebook and other social networking sites is to keep things positive. Nobody likes to hear complaints about things everybody has to do, such as "Ugh. I have to wake up for school." Likewise, fighting on Facebook only paints you in a bad light. If others are fighting, avoid commenting, even as a peacemaker. Instead, talk to them in person. As far as "unfriending," this is considered an extreme measure. If someone is being mean to you or causing stress for you online, by all means, unfriend them. But unfriending a true friend after a disagreement at school or a girlfriend after a breakup is considered overly dramatic.

As with anything, mistakes are sometimes made. According to a 2011 Marist College survey, one in five Americans report having posting something they later regretted on social networking sites. On Facebook and Twitter, you can delete a post, but people may have already seen it. Say for instance that your friend doesn't show up for your basketball game and your team loses. You post, "Nice of Thomas not to show up. Lazy as always, he overslept." A few minutes later, you realize that was a hurtful thing to post on Facebook, so you delete it. But did he see it? Did the team? Did the coach? It's best to take a

wait-and-see approach. You don't want to call extra attention to the regrettable post. Wait and find out who saw it, and then apologize to them in person. If on the other hand, you post something in a forum, such as a fantasy baseball league, you might not be able to delete the post. In that case apologize and let it blow over before you go back to the forum.

Texts, e-mails, and phone calls are more private ways of sharing. Don't forward a text or e-mail unless you've been asked to spread the word about something. At the same time, don't text or e-mail anything you wouldn't want forwarded or sent to somebody by mistake. Again, contentious conversations are best not conducted in writing. Things in writing just sound harsher. Pick up the phone, or better yet, talk in person.

Technology is often painted in a negative light. But

technology is only as good or bad as people make it. If things are going bad, step away from the technology. You may be tempted to check a troubling online conversation to determine how things will stand at school the next day. Instead, ask a parent to monitor the situation for you. He or she can help you deal with the brewing trouble, too. If used well, technology can help you connect with friends. The best post is: "Let's go do something."

MYTHS AND FACTS

Myth: To have friends, you must be one of the cool kids.
Fact: To have friends, you just have to be a good person to be around.

Myth: To be happy, you must have lots of friends.
Fact: Only one good friend is needed to be happy. Even people with lots of friends need one close friend to feel connected.

Myth: Cyberbullying is basically being mean to someone online.
Fact: Cyberbullying is a deliberate, hostile, and often repeated act online. The victim and perpetrator both must be children or teens. Being mean to someone online can quickly escalate into cyberbullying.

10 GREAT QUESTIONS TO ASK A GUIDANCE COUNSELOR

1. HOW DO I MAKE FRIENDS AT A NEW SCHOOL?

2. HOW DO I DEAL WITH SHYNESS WHEN TRYING TO TALK TO NEW PEOPLE?

3. HOW DO I KNOW THAT SOMEBODY IS A GOOD FRIEND?

4. HOW DO I HELP A FRIEND WHO'S GOING THROUGH HARD TIMES?

5. WHAT DO I DO IF I REALIZE MY FRIEND ISN'T A GOOD FRIEND?

6. WHAT DO I DO IF A FRIEND NO LONGER WANTS TO BE MY FRIEND?

7. WHAT IF I NO LONGER WANT TO BE SOMEONE'S FRIEND?

8. WHAT DO I DO WHEN MY GROUP OF FRIENDS IS FIGHTING?

9. WHAT DO I DO IF SOMETHING RUDE OR EMBARRASSING IS POSTED ABOUT ME ONLINE?

10. WHAT DO I DO IF I REGRET SOMETHING I POSTED ONLINE?

GLOSSARY

abuse Hurtful treatment, whether physical, emotional, or sexual.

acquaintance A person one knows, but not well.

bullying Hurtful or intimidating treatment of another person.

clique A small group of friends that tends to exclude others.

communication The act of sharing thoughts, feelings, and information by talking, body language, or writing.

conversationalist One who enjoys and is good at talking with and listening to others.

cyberbullying Deliberate, hostile, and often repeated attacks by a child or teen toward another child or teen online.

discreet Being careful about what is said.

extrovert One who derives energy from being with people.

friend A person whom one knows well and likes. It often implies time spent together.

introvert One who derives energy from being alone.

social media Web sites on which users share information, thoughts, or feelings.

social network Several people connected to each other through friendships, acquaintances, or common interests. In computers, the same type of connection, only online, or a Web site on which such connections can be made.

stress The mental or physical pressure felt because of an external situation.

trust The belief in someone's dependability to do the right thing.

values Principles, standards, and goals held by a person or group.

FOR MORE INFORMATION

Advocates for Youth
2000 M Street NW, Suite 750
Washington, DC 20036
(202) 419-3420
Web site: http://www.advocatesforyouth.org
Advocates for Youth helps young people make responsible decisions
about their health and sexuality.

American Medical Association
515 N. State Street
Chicago, IL 60654
(800) 621-8335
Web site: http://www.ama-assn.org
The American Medical Association provides information on a variety of
matters, including adolescent health.

Canadian Association for Adolescent Health
Section médecine de l'adolescence
Sainte-Justine Hospital
7th Floor, 2nd Bloc
3175 Côte Sainte-Catherine
Montreal, QC H3T 1C5
Canada
(514) 345-9959
Web site: http://www.acsa-caah.ca
The Canadian Association for Adolescent Health promotes health in
adolescents.

Gay Straight Alliance Network
1550 Bryant Street, Suite 800

San Francisco, CA 94103

(415) 552-4229

Web site: http://www.gsanetwork.org

The Gay Straight Alliance empowers students to fight homophobia in schools.

Web Sites

Due to the changing nature of Internet links, Rosen Publishing has developed an online list of Web sites related to the subject of this book. This site is updated regularly. Please use this link to access the list:

http://www.rosenlinks.com/r101/bbf

FOR FURTHER READING

Balliett, Blue. *Chasing Vermeer*. New York, NY: Scholastic, 2005.

Berman, Steve. *Speaking Out: LGBTQ Youth Stand Up*. Valley Falls, NY: Bold Strokes Books, 2011.

Boyett, Jason. *A Guy's Guide to Life: How to Become a Man in 224 Pages or Less*. Nashville, TN: Thomas Nelson, 2010.

Choron, Sandra, and Harry Choron. *The Book of Lists for Teens*. New York, NY: Mariner, 2002.

Covey, Sean. *The 6 Most Important Decisions You'll Ever Make: A Guide for Teens*. Clearwater, FL: Touchstone, 2006.

DiPiazza, Francesca Davis. *The Social Network: 600 Years of Social Networking in America*. Minneapolis, MN: Lerner, 2012.

Espeland, Pamela. *Life Lists for Teens: Tips, Steps, Hints, and How-Tos for Growing Up, Getting Along, Learning, and Having Fun*. Minneapolis, MN: Free Spirit, 2003.

Fox, Debbie. *Good-bye Bully Machine*. Minneapolis, MN: Free Spirit, 2005.

Lewis, Barbara. *What Do You Stand For? For Teens: A Guide to Building Character*. Minneapolis, MN: Free Spirit, 2005.

Macgregor, Cynthia. *Think for Yourself: A Kid's Guide to Solving Life's Dilemmas and Other Sticky Problems*. Montreal, Canada: Lobster Press, 2008.

Manivong, Laura. *Escaping the Tiger*. New York, NY: HarperCollins, 2010.

Markovics, Joyce. *Relationship Smarts: How to Navigate Dating, Friendships, Family Relationships, and More* (USA Today Teen Wise Guides: Time, Money, and Relationships). Minneapolis, MN: Lerner, 2012.

Mass, Wendy. *11 Birthdays*. New York, NY: Scholastic, 2009.

Pfeifer, Kate Gruenwald. *American Medical Association Boy's Guide to Becoming a Teen*. Hoboken, NJ: Jossey-Bass, 2006.

Romain, Trevor. *Cliques, Phonies, & Other Baloney*. Minneapolis, MN: Free Spirit, 1998.

Ryan, Peter. *Social Networking* (Digital & Information Literacy). New York, NY: Rosen Publishing, 2011.

Twain, Mark. *The Adventures of Tom Sawyer and Huckleberry Finn*. New York, NY: Signet Classics, 2002.

Van Draanen, Wendelin. *Flipped*. New York, NY: Knopf, 2010.

Verdick, Elizabeth, ed. *The Teen Survival Guide to Dating & Relating: Real-World Advice for Teens on Guys, Girls, Growing Up, and Getting Along*. Minneapolis, MN: Free Spirit, 2005.

BIBLIOGRAPHY

Brehony, Kathleen. *Living a Connected Life: Creating and Maintaining Relationships That Last.* New York, NY: Holt, 2003.

Bridges, John. *50 Things Every Young Gentleman Should Know: What to Do, When to Do It, and Why.* Nashville, TN: Rutledge Hill, 2006.

Elias, Maurice, Steven Tobias, and Brian Friedlander. *Raising Emotionally Intelligent Teenagers.* New York, NY: Harmony, 2002.

Epstein, Joseph. *Friendship: An Exposé.* New York, NY: Houghton Mifflin, 2006.

Feldhahn, Jeff, and Eric Rice. *For Young Men Only.* Colorado Springs, CO: Multnomah Books, 2008.

Fox, Annie. *Can You Relate?* Minneapolis, MN: Free Spirit, 1999.

Gaughan, Colleen. Interview. Social Media and Teens. September 21, 2011.

Goodstein, Anastasia. *Totally Wired: What Teens and Tweens Are Really Doing Online.* New York, NY: St. Martin's, 2007.

Handler, Cindy Schweich. "A Few Good Friends." *Ladies' Home Journal.* Retrieved September 28, 2011 (http://www.lhj.com/relationships/family/raising-kids/a-few-good-friends).

Haynes, Cyndi. *The Book of Friendship.* Kansas City, MO: Andrews-McMeel, 2001.

Horchow, Roger, and Sally Horchow. *The Art of Friendship: 70 Simple Rules for Making Meaningful Connections.* New York, NY: Quirk, 2005.

Jackson, Lindsay. *101 Things Teens Should Know.* Kansas City, MO: Andrews-McMeel, 2002.

Martinet, Jeanne. *Life Is Friends: A Complete Guide to the Lost Art of Connecting in Person.* New York, NY: Abrams, 2009.

Patrick, Maggy. "Internet Regrets Hit One in Five Americans Who Post on Social Media." *ABC News*, July 27, 2011. Retrieved September 28, 2011 (http://abcnews.go.com/Technology/internet-regrets-social-media-users/story?id=14162983).

Pogrebin, Letty Cottin. *Among Friends: Who We Like, Why We Like Them, and What We Do with Them.* New York, NY: McGraw-Hill, 1987.

Rath, Tom. *Vital Friends: The People You Can't Afford to Live Without.* New York, NY: Gallup, 2006.

Weeks, Linton. "Social Networks: Thinking of the Children." NPR, July 11, 2011. Retrieved September 28, 2011 (http://www.npr.org/2011/07/11/137670547/social-networks-thinking-of-the-children).

INDEX

About the Author

Bridget Heos is the author of several young adult nonfiction titles on topics ranging from biographies to science to states. Prior to being an author for teens, she was a newspaper reporter and freelance journalist. She lives in Kansas City with her husband and three sons.

Photo Credits

Cover, p. 1 © istockphoto.com/Jane Norton; pp. 3 (top), 13 © John Powell/TopFoto/The Image Works; pp. 3 (bottom), 22 Comstock Images/Thinkstock; pp. 4–5, 9 Jupiterimages/Brand X Pictures/Thinkstock; pp. 6, 15, 21, 29 © istockphoto.com/4x6; p. 7 Creatas Images/Creatas/Getty Images; p. 16 Comstock/Thinkstock; p. 19 Image Source/Thinkstock; p. 23 Michael Matisse/Photodisc/Thinkstock; p. 26 Jupiterimages/Comstock/Thinkstock; p. 30 © Giovanni Mereghetti/Marka/SuperStock; p. 31 © Bill Aron/PhotoEdit; p. 34 Eugenia-Petrenko/Shutterstock; interior graphics © istockphoto .com/kemie; back cover background, interior graphics © istockphoto .com/Stereohype.

Designer: Michael Moy; Editor: Bethany Bryan;
Photo Researcher: Marty Levick